SO WHICH PAGE ARE WE SUPPOSED TO BE ON?

WHADDYA MEAN, WHICH PAGE? I THOUGHT WE WERE TO BE ON ALL THE PAGES. ISN'T THIS THE COCKROACH STUFF BOOK?

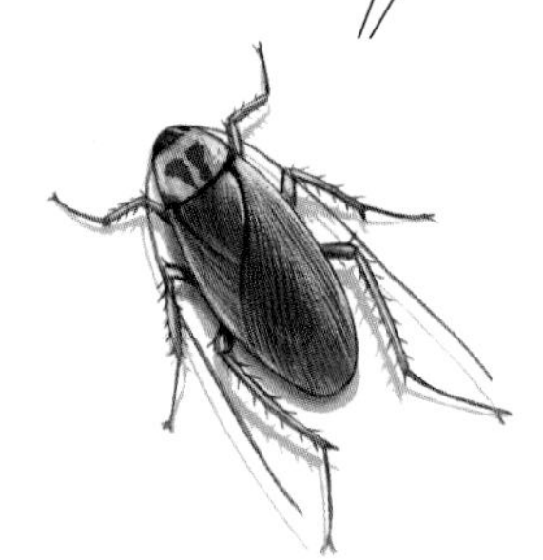

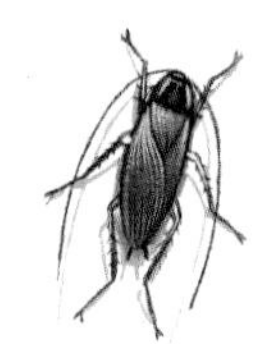

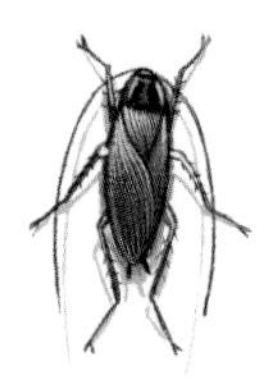

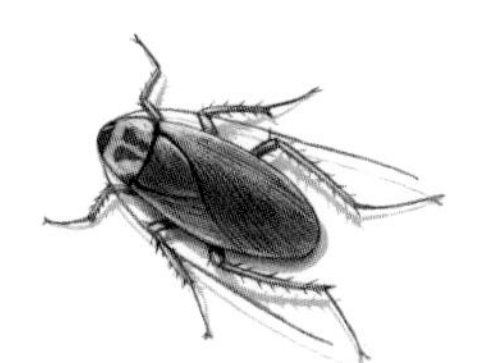

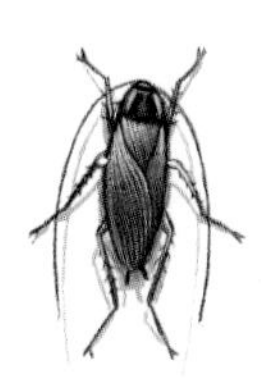

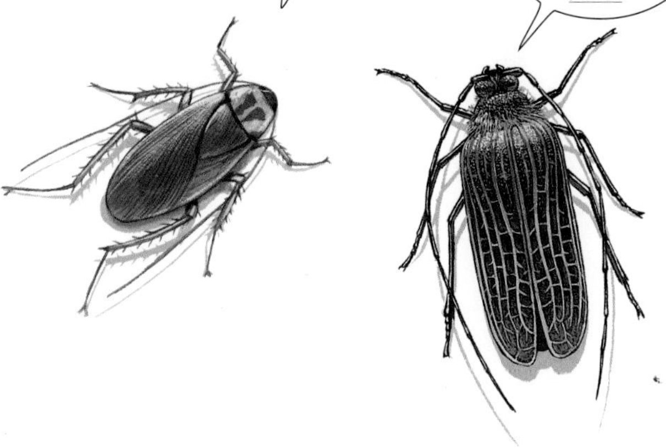
BOY, YOU'RE AN UGLY-LOOKING COCKROACH. DAVE REALLY DID A LOUSY JOB OF DRAWING YOU, DIDN'T HE?
I'M NOT A COCKROACH, YOU IDIOT. I'M A BEETLE!

This book is dedicated to all New Zealand cockroaches and their countless relatives throughout the world

OH, ISN'T THAT SWEET?

Published by Scholastic New Zealand Limited, 1999
Private Bag 94407, Greenmount, Auckland 1730, New Zealand.

Scholastic Australia Pty Limited
PO Box 579, Gosford, NSW 2250, Australia.

Scholastic Inc
555 Broadway, New York, NY 10012-3999, USA.

Scholastic Limited
1-19 New Oxford Street, London, WC1A 1NU, England.

Scholastic Canada Limited
123 Newkirk Road, Richmond Hill, Ontario L4C 3G5, Canada.

Scholastic Mexico
Bretana 99, Col. Zacahuitzco, 03550 Mexico D.F., Mexico.

Scholastic India Pte Limited
29 Udyog Vihar, Phase-1, Gurgaon-122 016, Haryana, India.

Scholastic Hong Kong
Room 601-2, Tung Shung Hing Commercial Centre,
20-22 Granville Road, Kowloon, Hong Kong.

ISBN 978-1-86943-405-2

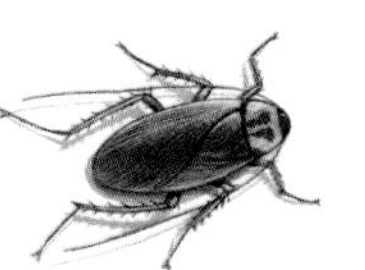

9 8 7 6 5 4 0 1 2 3 4 5 / 1

Edited by Penny Springthorpe
Printed in Hong Kong

DON'T LIKE HER, THEN.

WILDLIFE STUFF

DAVE GUNSON

SCHOLASTIC
AUCKLAND SYDNEY NEW YORK LONDON TORONTO
MEXICO CITY NEW DELHI HONG KONG

an average ant
G'DAY!
New Zealand has about 10 native ant species and about 23 introduced species. The average ant weighs just 5mg, so it would take about 1,800,000 ants to equal the weight of New Zealand's heaviest bird, the royal albatross, which can weigh up to 9kg. Many ants like to feed on honeydew—a sweet liquid secreted by aphids and other insects.
The albatross flies by making clever use of gliding in wind currents—soaring and swooping to maintain height and speed. An albatross can cover well over 5,000km on a single feeding journey lasting two weeks, and can spend up to a year at sea without ever touching land.
Many ants have a distinctive smell. This comes from the formic acid in their bodies.
WHERE'S THE COCKROACHES THEN?
AW, PHEW!
SORRY ABOUT THAT.
WHAT'S THAT SMELL?
royal albatross
THAT'S 1,800,001! ONE TOO MANY. YOU'LL HAVE TO GET OFF, ANDY.
AW, STINK!

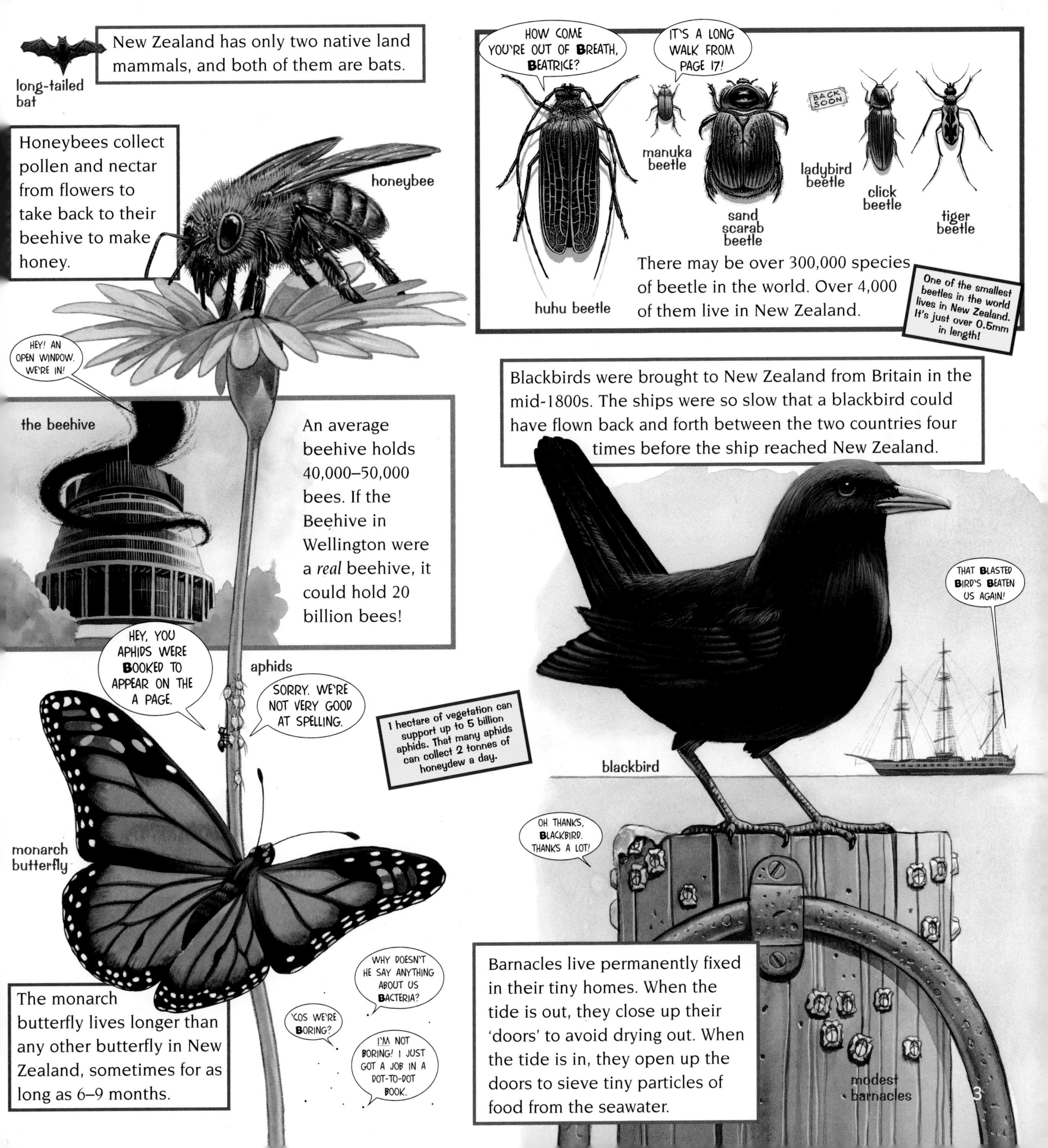

New Zealand has only two native land mammals, and both of them are bats.

Honeybees collect pollen and nectar from flowers to take back to their beehive to make honey.

An average beehive holds 40,000–50,000 bees. If the Beehive in Wellington were a *real* beehive, it could hold 20 billion bees!

1 hectare of vegetation can support up to 5 billion aphids. That many aphids can collect 2 tonnes of honeydew a day.

The monarch butterfly lives longer than any other butterfly in New Zealand, sometimes for as long as 6–9 months.

There may be over 300,000 species of beetle in the world. Over 4,000 of them live in New Zealand.

One of the smallest beetles in the world lives in New Zealand. It's just over 0.5mm in length!

Blackbirds were brought to New Zealand from Britain in the mid-1800s. The ships were so slow that a blackbird could have flown back and forth between the two countries four times before the ship reached New Zealand.

Barnacles live permanently fixed in their tiny homes. When the tide is out, they close up their 'doors' to avoid drying out. When the tide is in, they open up the doors to sieve tiny particles of food from the seawater.

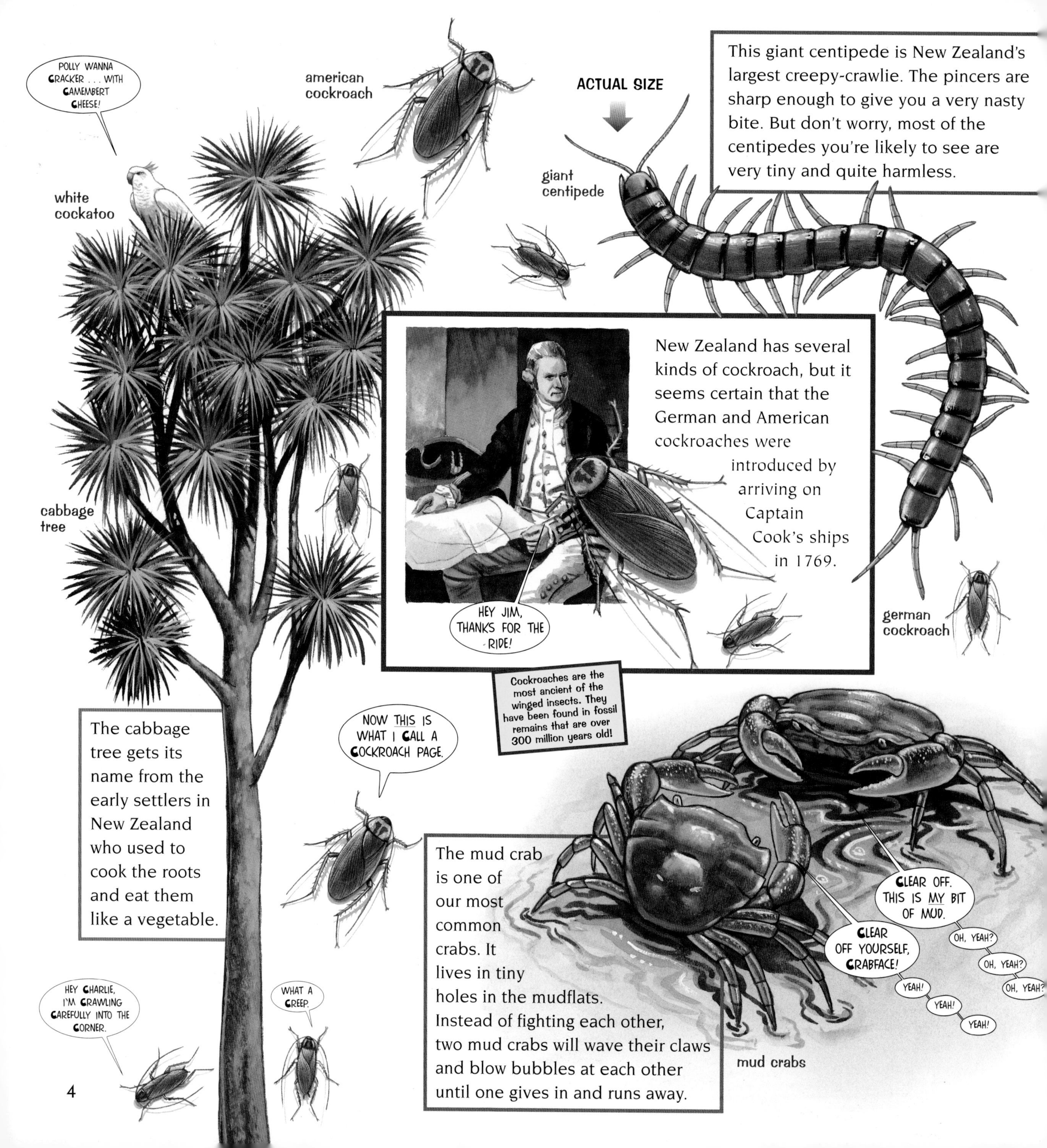

This giant centipede is New Zealand's largest creepy-crawlie. The pincers are sharp enough to give you a very nasty bite. But don't worry, most of the centipedes you're likely to see are very tiny and quite harmless.

New Zealand has several kinds of cockroach, but it seems certain that the German and American cockroaches were introduced by arriving on Captain Cook's ships in 1769.

Cockroaches are the most ancient of the winged insects. They have been found in fossil remains that are over 300 million years old!

The cabbage tree gets its name from the early settlers in New Zealand who used to cook the roots and eat them like a vegetable.

The mud crab is one of our most common crabs. It lives in tiny holes in the mudflats. Instead of fighting each other, two mud crabs will wave their claws and blow bubbles at each other until one gives in and runs away.

Long ago, New Zealand had lots of different dinosaurs. One was like the diplodocus pictured here. Imagine what it would be like to see one alive today! Other types included ankylosaurs, megalosaurs, carnosaurs, hypsilophodonts and the velociraptor *deinonychus*.

Dinosaurs died out about 65 million years ago—about 60 million years before the first humans appeared.

Editor's note: No, Dave, you *can't* make this a scratch 'n' sniff page!

The daddy-long-legs is perfectly harmless, as it has no poison glands at all. When it lays its eggs, it carries them around in a small ball until they hatch. If the web is disturbed, the spider does a strange dance, shaking so violently that it becomes a blur.

Several species of deer were introduced to New Zealand in the middle of the last century. In some parts of the country they are regarded as pests because they damage native plants and forest vegetation by grazing on young seedlings.

Daisies form one of the largest plant groups in New Zealand. There are about 60 different types of mountain daisy alone.

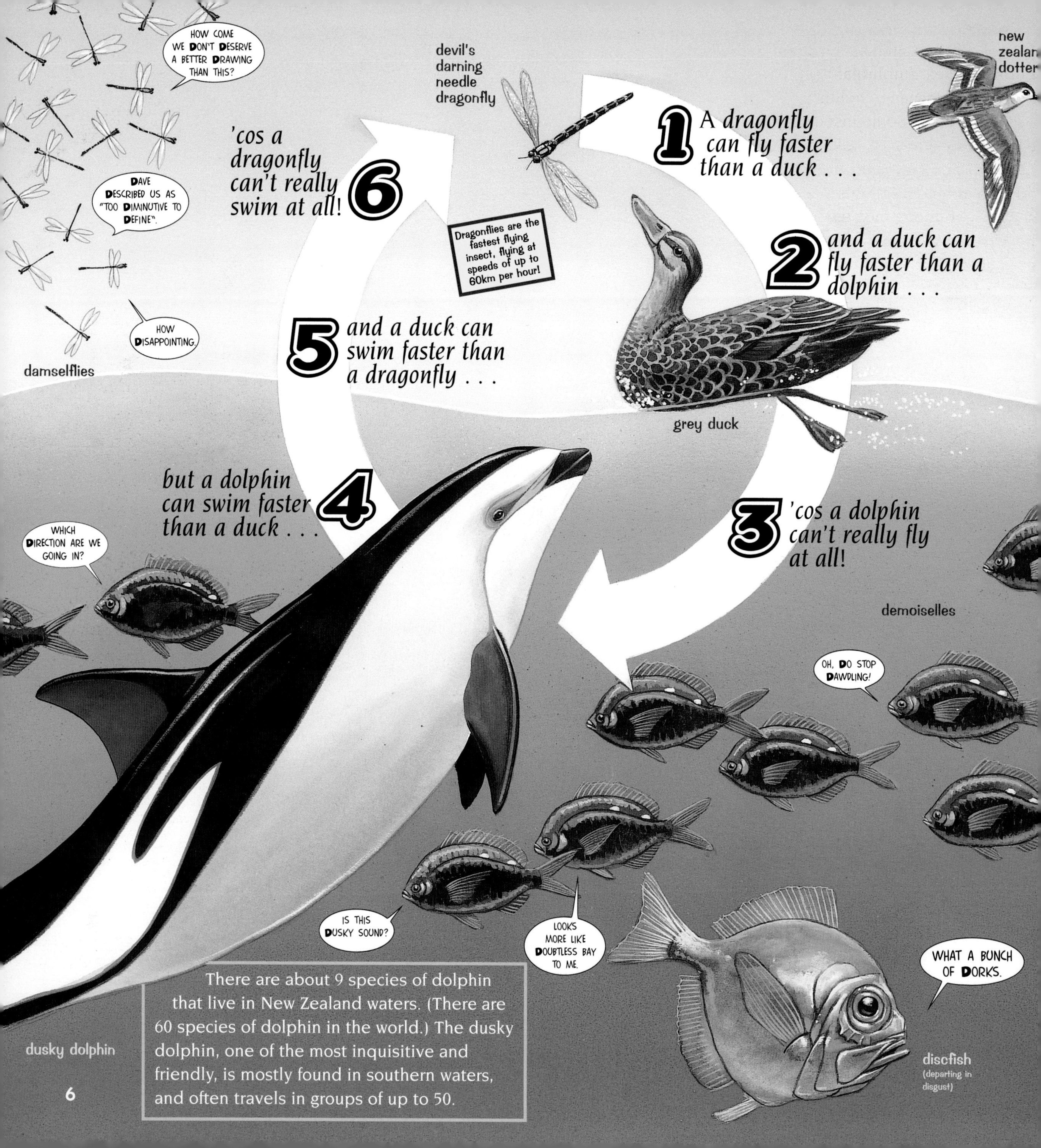

There are about 9 species of dolphin that live in New Zealand waters. (There are 60 species of dolphin in the world.) The dusky dolphin, one of the most inquisitive and friendly, is mostly found in southern waters, and often travels in groups of up to 50.

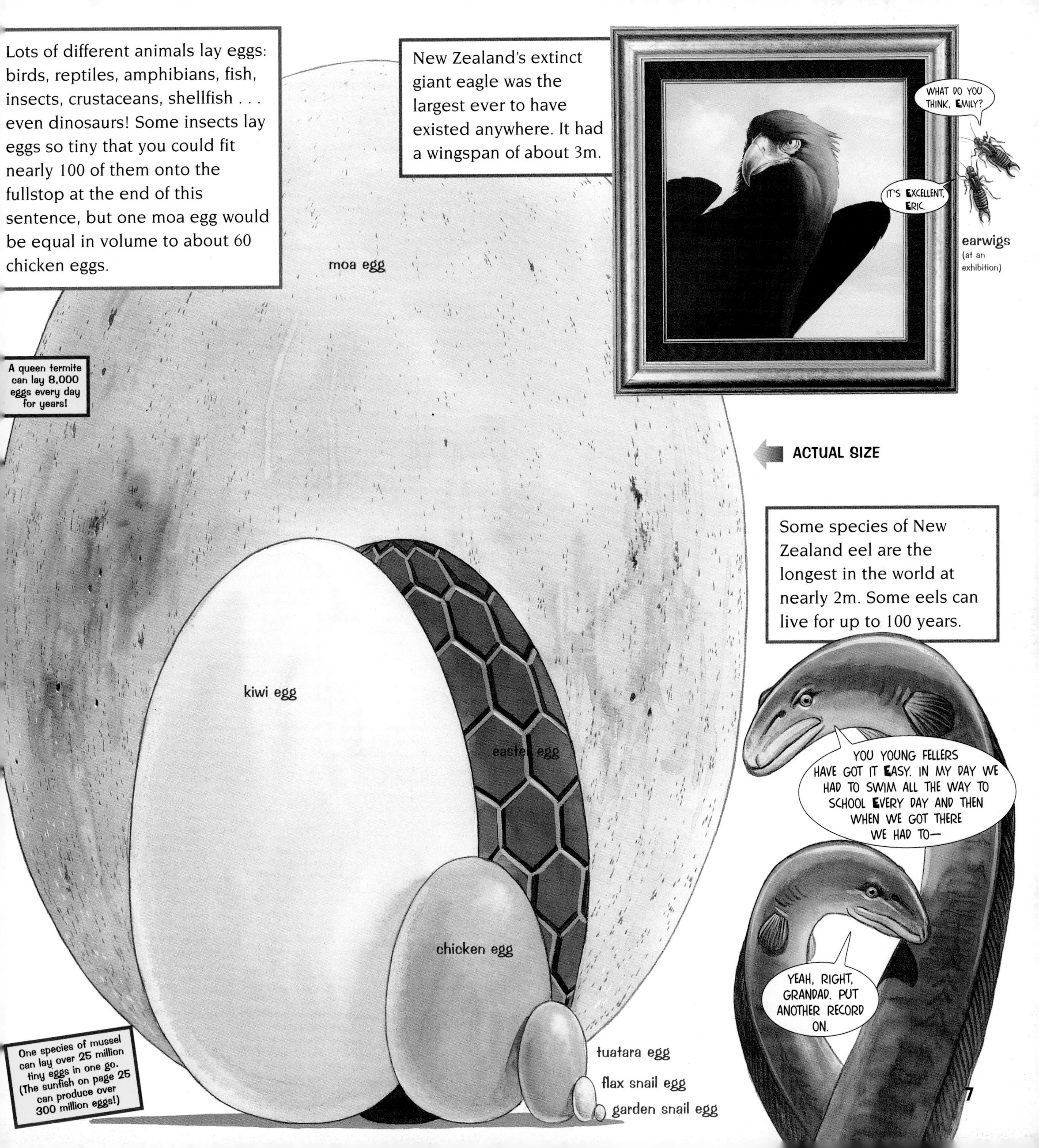

Lots of different animals lay eggs: birds, reptiles, amphibians, fish, insects, crustaceans, shellfish . . . even dinosaurs! Some insects lay eggs so tiny that you could fit nearly 100 of them onto the fullstop at the end of this sentence, but one moa egg would be equal in volume to about 60 chicken eggs.
New Zealand's extinct giant eagle was the largest ever to have existed anywhere. It had a wingspan of about 3m.
WHAT DO YOU THINK, EMILY?
IT'S EXCELLENT, ERIC.
earwigs
(at an exhibition)
moa egg
A queen termite can lay 8,000 eggs every day for years!
ACTUAL SIZE
Some species of New Zealand eel are the longest in the world at nearly 2m. Some eels can live for up to 100 years.
kiwi egg
easter egg
YOU YOUNG FELLERS HAVE GOT IT EASY. IN MY DAY WE HAD TO SWIM ALL THE WAY TO SCHOOL EVERY DAY AND THEN WHEN WE GOT THERE WE HAD TO—
chicken egg
YEAH, RIGHT, GRANDAD. PUT ANOTHER RECORD ON.
One species of mussel can lay over 25 million tiny eggs in one go. (The sunfish on page 25 can produce over 300 million eggs!)
tuatara egg
flax snail egg
garden snail egg

There are more than 1,000 species of snails in New Zealand, and even the fastest of them would take about 2 hours to cover 100m. A human can walk the distance in about 1 minute.

The flax snail is not a fast snail. It can live for years in practically the same place and hardly move any distance at all. The flax snail does not live on or eat flax plants; it was given its name because it is often found living in the far north, close to coastal flax plants.

New Zealand has lots of different types of ferns. The tallest is the mamaku, which can grow to 12m, and sometimes as high as 20m. The smallest fern is only 25mm high (about half the length of your little finger).

New Zealand native frogs are all quite small and rare, and are among the most primitive types in the world. Their young pass the tadpole stage while still inside the egg, and emerge as tiny froglets.

The fantail lives in the forest fringes, and feeds by catching flies and insects while flying in and out of the foliage.

There are nearly 2,000 different kinds of flea. Fleas can jump up to 130 times their own height. That would be like a human jumping 240m into the air.

The largest fungus found in New Zealand is a bracket fungus that grows on trees and can reach over 1m in diameter.

This fly agaric mushroom is one of thousands of fungus species found in New Zealand (and in fairytales).

* If you see this mushroom, don't touch it. It's poisonous!
Dave

Geckos cannot blink, so they have to clean their eyes with a lick of their tongues.

Nearly all gecko species found around the world lay eggs, but New Zealand geckos are different. They give birth to live young. There are nearly 30 species found in New Zealand and are either grey-brown (which means they are mostly active by night) or green (which means they are active by day).

Glow-worms emit a tiny blue light to attract small flying insects into a trap of sticky threads. You can see glow-worms in many caves and bush areas at night.

Glow-worms aren't worms at all! They're the larval stage of a tiny fly.

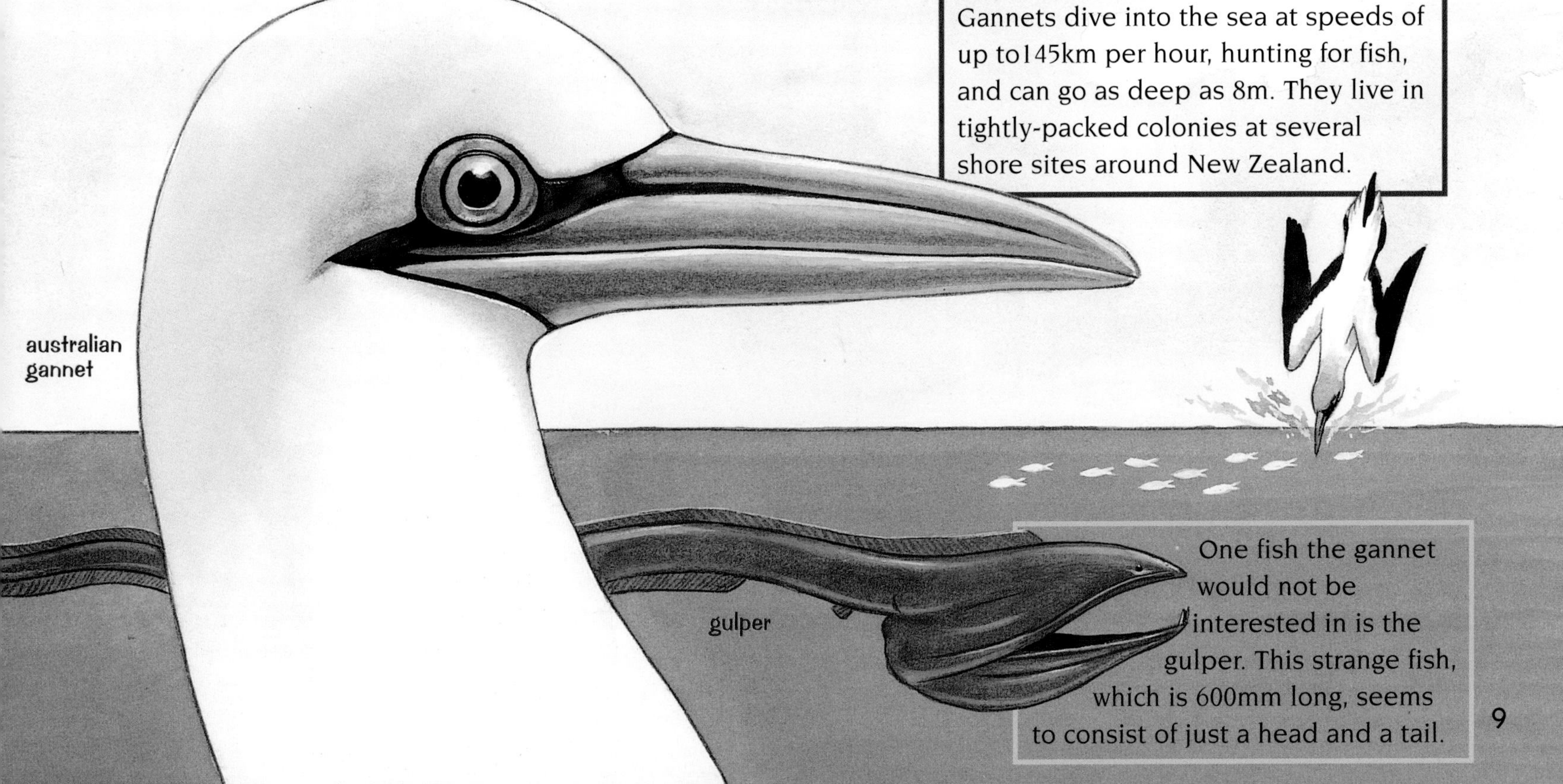

Gannets dive into the sea at speeds of up to145km per hour, hunting for fish, and can go as deep as 8m. They live in tightly-packed colonies at several shore sites around New Zealand.

One fish the gannet would not be interested in is the gulper. This strange fish, which is 600mm long, seems to consist of just a head and a tail.

The now-extinct huia was one of our most distinctive birds. The male had an ordinary bill, but the female had a long curved bill that she used to break open decayed wood to get at the fat grubs of the huhu beetle.

The harrier is our largest bird of prey and will sometimes be seen at the roadside feeding on carrion (road kill).

Four types of heron live in New Zealand. The white heron breeds only at Okarito, in the South Island.

Hedgehogs were first introduced into New Zealand in Canterbury in 1870. There are now more hedgehogs here than in Great Britain, where they came from, and they've become quite a pest in some parts of the country.

The common housefly, shown here many times its actual size, feeds by vomiting on its food to soften it. Then it sucks up the mess! The housefly enjoys the variety of tasty bits and pieces it can find in an ordinary house, and it will also look for any sweet or rotting food outside the house. It transfers dirt and bacteria as it forages back and forth. Houseflies probably arrived in New Zealand during the 1800s as maggots in food kept in ships' holds.

LENGTH 6mm
WINGSPAN 14mm
WEIGHT under 0.25g
AIRSPEED 250mm per second
WINGBEAT 190 per second
LIFESPAN 2–12 weeks
BACTERIA 100–350 million

Hermit crabs have soft bodies with no protective armour. They make their homes inside shells that have been abandoned by other creatures, and as they grow they must move to larger and larger shells. If a hermit crab is threatened, it can retreat into its shell and block the entrance with its large right nipper.

The hagfish is a very primitive fish. It is about 1m long and has no proper fins, eyes, bony skeleton or jaws. It hunts dead or living fish by smell and then attaches itself, sucker-like, to eat its prey. If it's disturbed, it produces huge amounts of sticky slime from mucus glands on its sides.

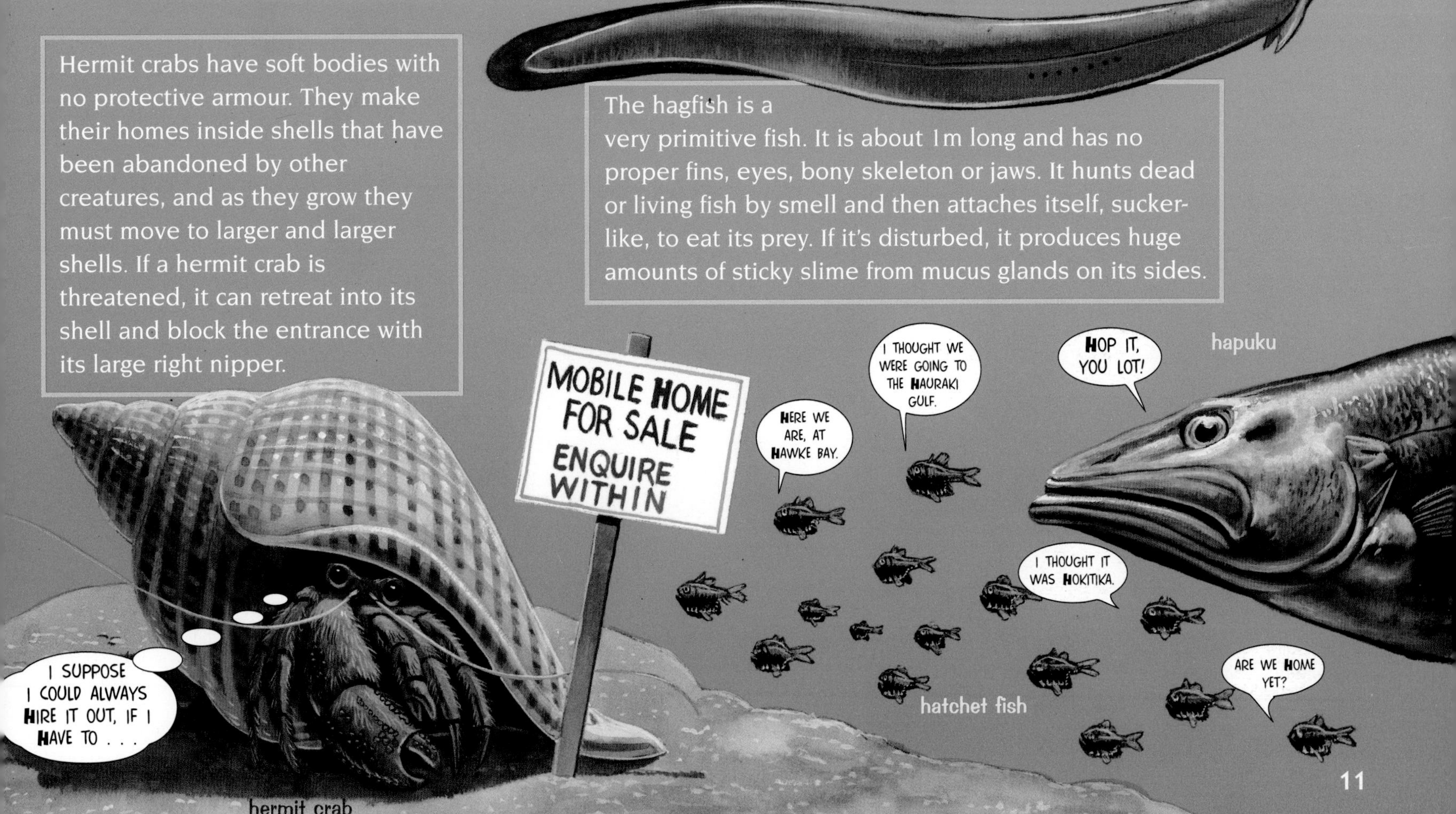

Isopods (also called slaters or woodlice) feed on dead and decaying plant and animal material. They are some of nature's cleaners and tidy-uppers. They may look like insects, but actually they're crustaceans. (An insect always has 6 legs, but an isopod has 14.)

A group of jellyfish is called a smuck (and that's exactly the sound a jellyfish makes if it's dropped on the sand).

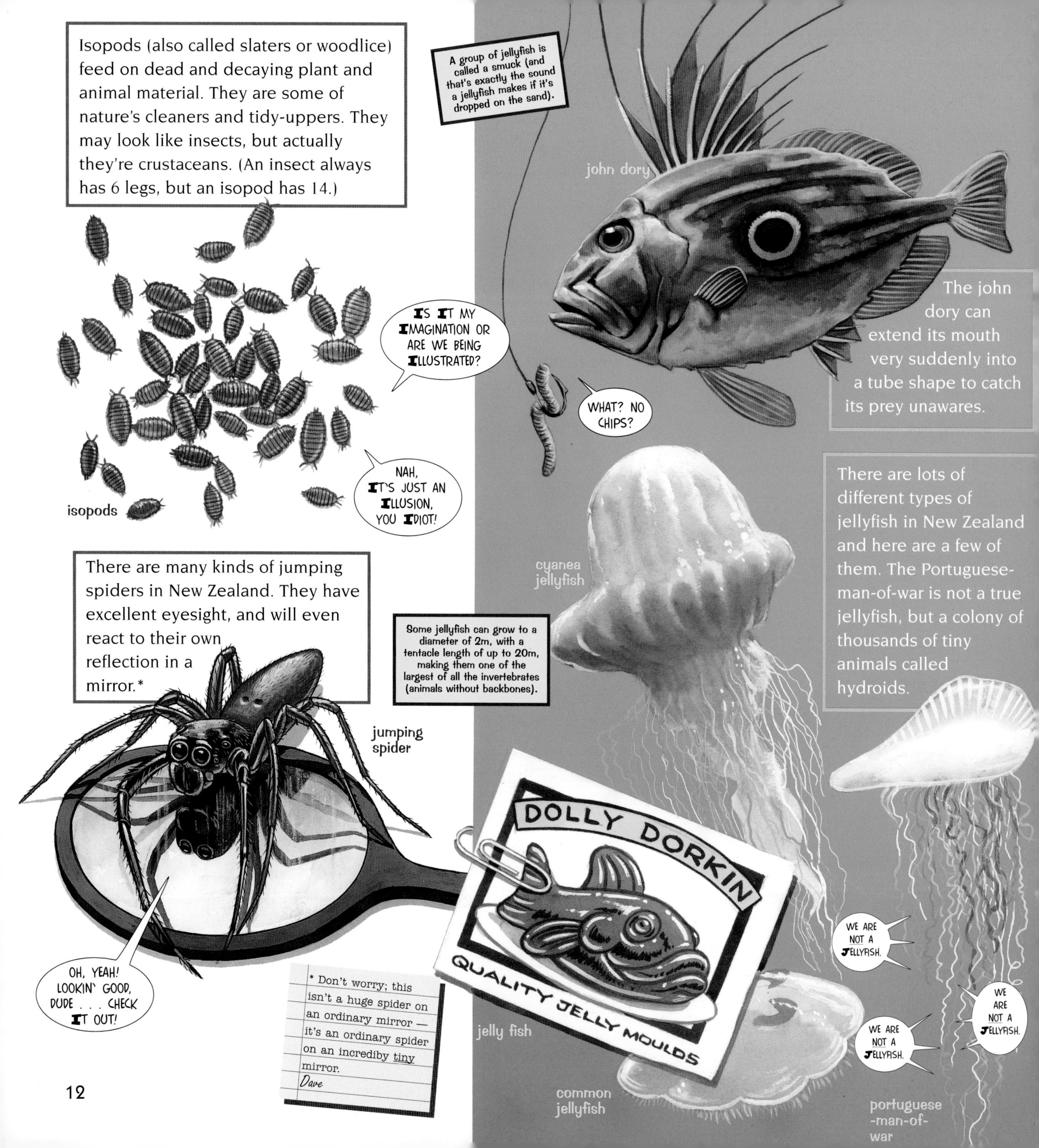

The john dory can extend its mouth very suddenly into a tube shape to catch its prey unawares.

There are lots of different types of jellyfish in New Zealand and here are a few of them. The Portuguese-man-of-war is not a true jellyfish, but a colony of thousands of tiny animals called hydroids.

There are many kinds of jumping spiders in New Zealand. They have excellent eyesight, and will even react to their own reflection in a mirror.*

Some jellyfish can grow to a diameter of 2m, with a tentacle length of up to 20m, making them one of the largest of all the invertebrates (animals without backbones).

* Don't worry; this isn't a huge spider on an ordinary mirror — it's an ordinary spider on an incrediby tiny mirror.
Dave

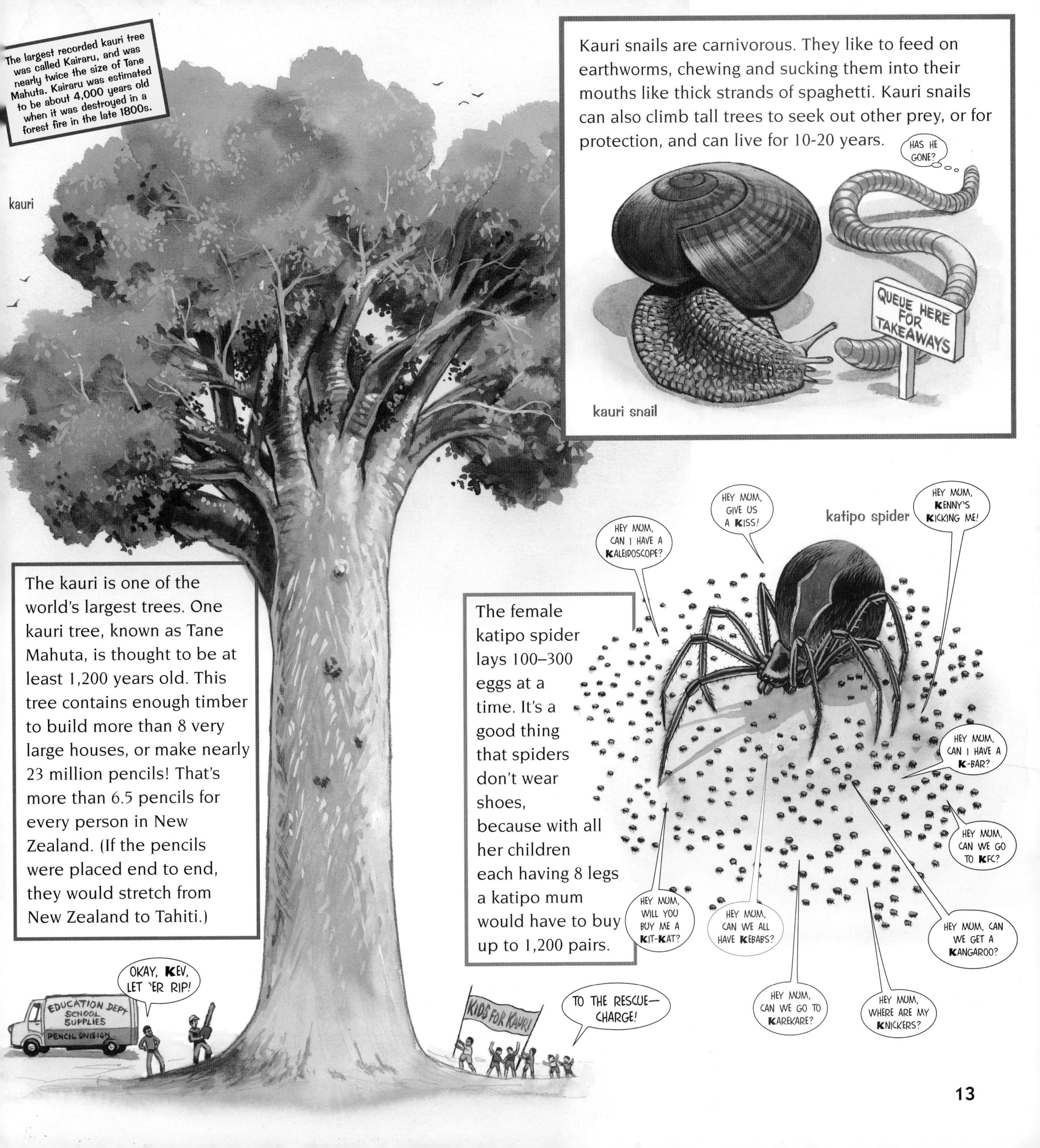

The largest recorded kauri tree was called Kairaru, and was nearly twice the size of Tane Mahuta. Kairaru was estimated to be about 4,000 years old when it was destroyed in a forest fire in the late 1800s.

Kauri snails are carnivorous. They like to feed on earthworms, chewing and sucking them into their mouths like thick strands of spaghetti. Kauri snails can also climb tall trees to seek out other prey, or for protection, and can live for 10-20 years.

The kauri is one of the world's largest trees. One kauri tree, known as Tane Mahuta, is thought to be at least 1,200 years old. This tree contains enough timber to build more than 8 very large houses, or make nearly 23 million pencils! That's more than 6.5 pencils for every person in New Zealand. (If the pencils were placed end to end, they would stretch from New Zealand to Tahiti.)

The female katipo spider lays 100–300 eggs at a time. It's a good thing that spiders don't wear shoes, because with all her children each having 8 legs a katipo mum would have to buy up to 1,200 pairs.

The kahikatea is New Zealand's tallest tree, often reaching more than 60m in height. They can live for more than 500 years. Many other plants will grow on the trunk and branches of the kahikatea, including mosses, liverworts, kiekie, ferns, seed plants and lichens.

The kakapo is the heaviest parrot in the world. It can't fly, but it will climb trees and then glide clumsily back to the ground. The kakapo is thought to live for about 50 years.

Kingfishers are most common in coastal areas and open country. They do eat fish, but they also eat insects, worms, mice, lizards and even small birds.

The kiwi is one of New Zealand's most famous national symbols. It is active mostly at night, searching out its food by probing the litter on the forest floor with its long beak. Its nostrils are right at the tip of its beak, and its sense of smell is excellent. Of all the birds in the world, the kiwi is famous for laying the largest egg compared to body size. The egg equals about 25 percent of the bird's body weight.

The kea is the clown prince of New Zealand parrots. They're very inquisitive and will often destroy any belongings left out by climbers and tourists. They'll even strip the trim and accessories from parked cars! Some kea enjoy 'skiing' down the corrugated roofs of trampers' huts.

The bladder kelp is one of the fastest-growing plants in the world. It can grow at the rate of 500mm per day.

The kaka is a close relative of the kea. This parrot's favourite foods are honeydew sap from beech trees and the kanuka long-horn beetle.

The kokako is a very ancient bird type, and is related to the now-extinct huia. Only small numbers of kokako remain in North Island forests and offshore islands. These birds cannot fly very well, and prefer to scramble and jump from branch to branch. Kokako live for about 20 years.

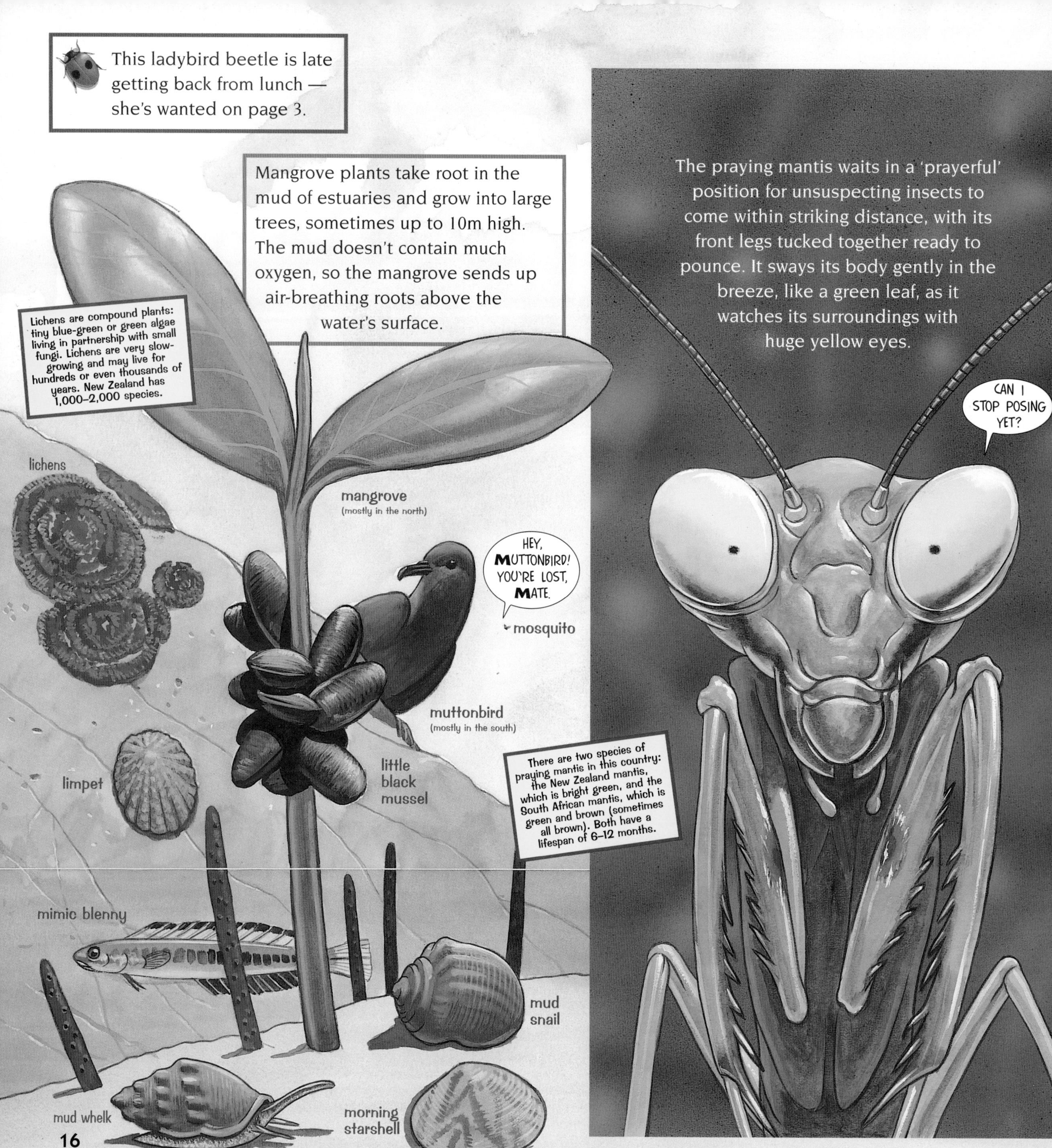
This ladybird beetle is late getting back from lunch — she's wanted on page 3.
Mangrove plants take root in the mud of estuaries and grow into large trees, sometimes up to 10m high. The mud doesn't contain much oxygen, so the mangrove sends up air-breathing roots above the water's surface.
Lichens are compound plants: tiny blue-green or green algae living in partnership with small fungi. Lichens are very slow-growing and may live for hundreds or even thousands of years. New Zealand has 1,000–2,000 species.
lichens
mangrove
(mostly in the north)
HEY, MUTTONBIRD! YOU'RE LOST, MATE.
mosquito
muttonbird
(mostly in the south)
limpet
little black mussel
mimic blenny
mud snail
mud whelk
morning starshell
The praying mantis waits in a 'prayerful' position for unsuspecting insects to come within striking distance, with its front legs tucked together ready to pounce. It sways its body gently in the breeze, like a green leaf, as it watches its surroundings with huge yellow eyes.
CAN I STOP POSING YET?
There are two species of praying mantis in this country: the New Zealand mantis, which is bright green, and the South African mantis, which is green and brown (sometimes all brown). Both have a lifespan of 6–12 months.

The morepork is our most common owl, and its call can be heard in urban as well as country areas. Its prey includes rats and mice.

The largest moth in the world is the great owlet moth from the USA, with a wingspan of 360mm.

If a moth wanted to fly to the mightiest nightlight of all—the moon—it would take 9 years to get there and back. (Unfortunately no moth lives for more than a few months.)

The moa was one of the biggest birds ever to have existed in the world. The largest species of moa weighed over 250kg and stood 3m tall when upright. Moa died out hundreds of years ago, so the only way you'll get to see one now is in a museum.

Most of the 1700 moth species in New Zealand are active during the night, but the magpie moth prefers to fly in the daytime.

Early settlers used to make tea from manuka leaves. The plant is also an important food source and home for geckos, moths, bees and other insects, including the manuka beetle.

There are over 600 species of millipede in New Zealand. They can be as big as 100mm, or as small as 3–4mm, like this: ∫ They like to munch on plant material, including mosses.

Orca (killer whales) can be seen all around New Zealand's coast. Armed with 40–50 strong peg-like teeth, they prey on a wide variety of ocean dwellers, including stingrays and other fish, seals, penguins and dolphins. A pack of orca can hunt and kill larger prey, even the huge blue whale. Orca can live for about 80 years.

Orange roughy normally live more than 1km below the sea's surface and may live for up to 150 years.

The nikau is the only palm tree native to New Zealand. It grows up to 10m in height. The tree produces bright red berries, which the New Zealand wood pigeon loves to eat.

The octopus uses the hundreds of suckers on its 8 arms to catch crustaceans, fish and mulluscs. Expelling water at great pressure from its siphon gives the octopus a sort of underwater jet propulsion!

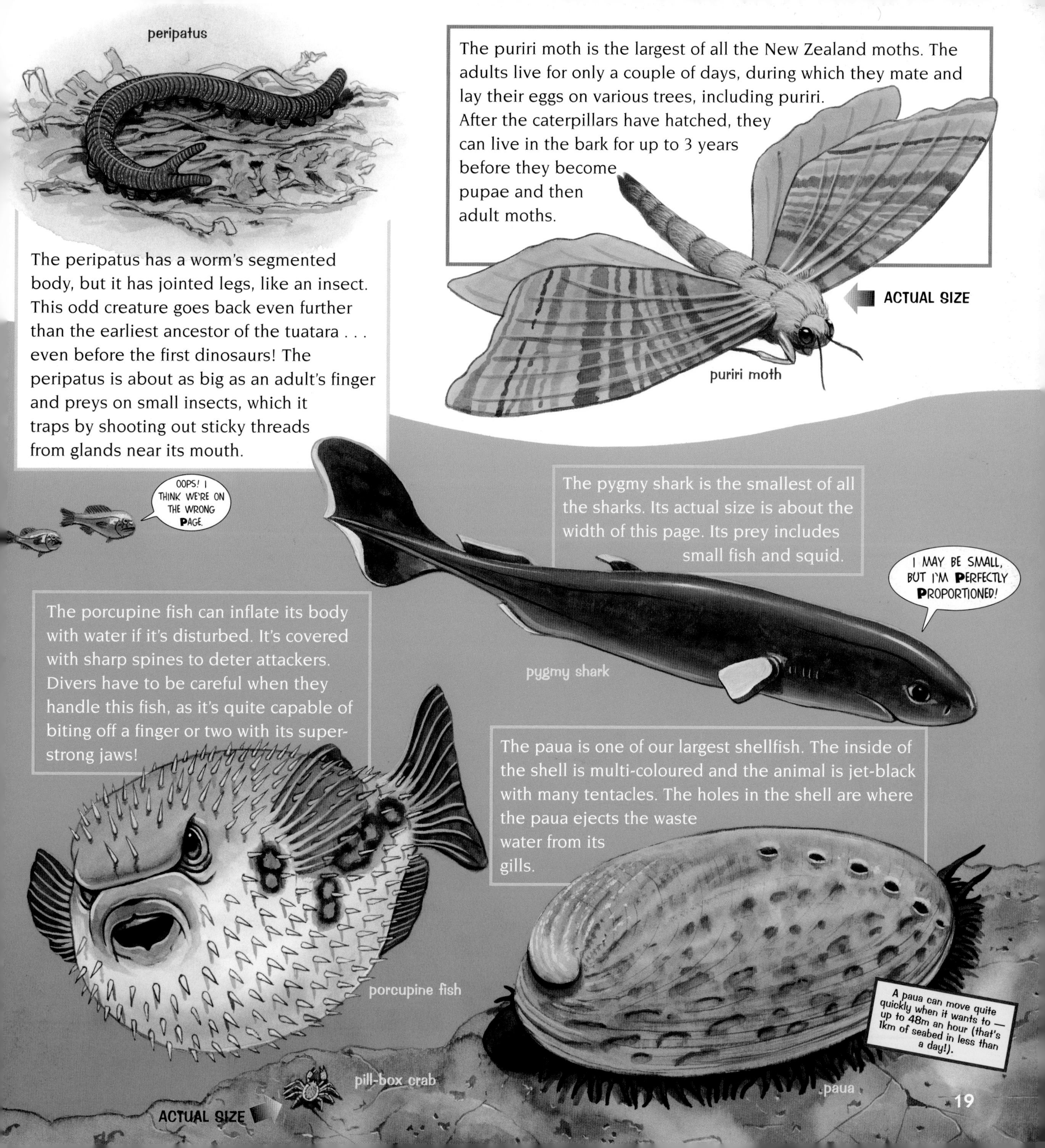

The peripatus has a worm's segmented body, but it has jointed legs, like an insect. This odd creature goes back even further than the earliest ancestor of the tuatara . . . even before the first dinosaurs! The peripatus is about as big as an adult's finger and preys on small insects, which it traps by shooting out sticky threads from glands near its mouth.

The puriri moth is the largest of all the New Zealand moths. The adults live for only a couple of days, during which they mate and lay their eggs on various trees, including puriri. After the caterpillars have hatched, they can live in the bark for up to 3 years before they become pupae and then adult moths.

The pygmy shark is the smallest of all the sharks. Its actual size is about the width of this page. Its prey includes small fish and squid.

The porcupine fish can inflate its body with water if it's disturbed. It's covered with sharp spines to deter attackers. Divers have to be careful when they handle this fish, as it's quite capable of biting off a finger or two with its super-strong jaws!

The paua is one of our largest shellfish. The inside of the shell is multi-coloured and the animal is jet-black with many tentacles. The holes in the shell are where the paua ejects the waste water from its gills.

Many penguin species live in the New Zealand region, including the endangered yellow-eyed penguin. The little blue penguin is the smallest species of all, at just 300–400mm tall, and is also the most common. The little blue penguin will make nests anywhere near the coast, even under houses! The extinct giant penguin was almost as tall as a full-grown person.

Pukeko live near wetlands and swamps, where they feed on insects and other small animals. A pukeko uses its feet like a parrot and grasps its food while eating. These birds sometimes live in communities and share nests, where all help to raise the chicks.

An emperor penguin has been recorded diving in the sea to a depth of 450m!

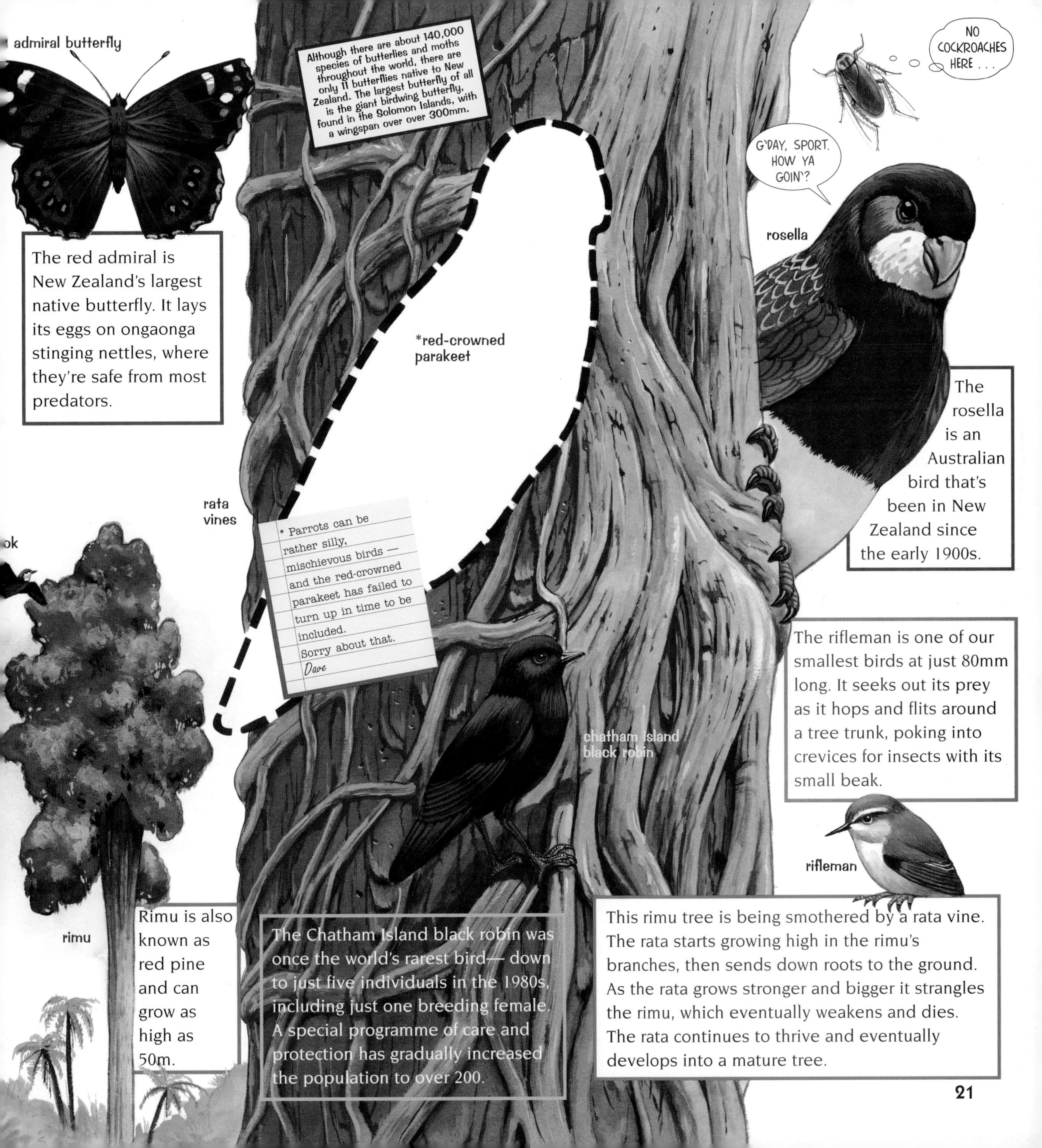

Although there are about 140,000 species of butterflies and moths throughout the world, there are only 11 butterflies native to New Zealand. The largest butterfly of all is the giant birdwing butterfly, found in the Solomon Islands, with a wingspan over over 300mm.

The red admiral is New Zealand's largest native butterfly. It lays its eggs on ongaonga stinging nettles, where they're safe from most predators.

* Parrots can be rather silly, mischievous birds — and the red-crowned parakeet has failed to turn up in time to be included.
Sorry about that.
Dave

The rosella is an Australian bird that's been in New Zealand since the early 1900s.

The rifleman is one of our smallest birds at just 80mm long. It seeks out its prey as it hops and flits around a tree trunk, poking into crevices for insects with its small beak.

Rimu is also known as red pine and can grow as high as 50m.

The Chatham Island black robin was once the world's rarest bird— down to just five individuals in the 1980s, including just one breeding female. A special programme of care and protection has gradually increased the population to over 200.

This rimu tree is being smothered by a rata vine. The rata starts growing high in the rimu's branches, then sends down roots to the ground. As the rata grows stronger and bigger it strangles the rimu, which eventually weakens and dies. The rata continues to thrive and eventually develops into a mature tree.

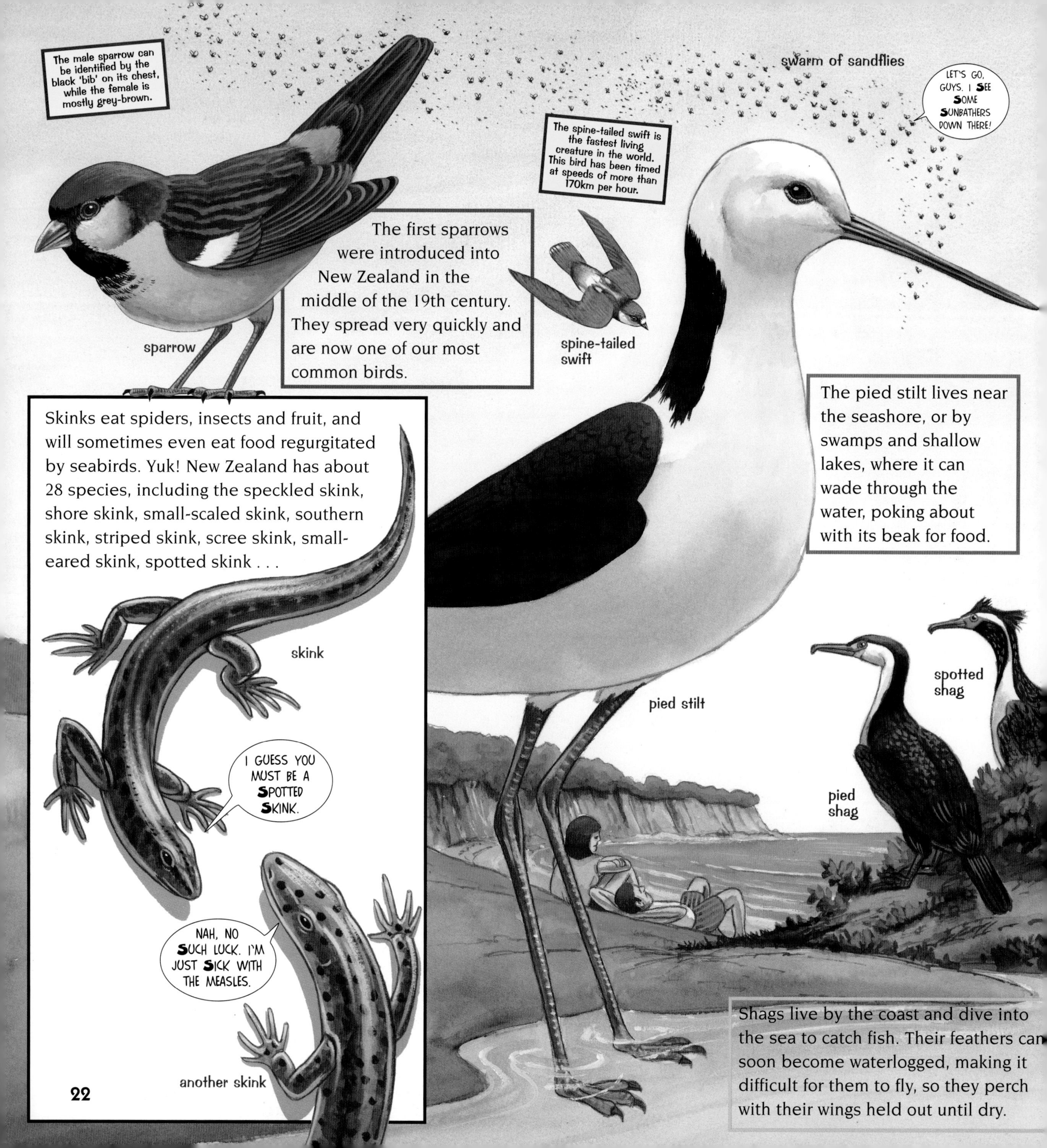

The first sparrows were introduced into New Zealand in the middle of the 19th century. They spread very quickly and are now one of our most common birds.

The pied stilt lives near the seashore, or by swamps and shallow lakes, where it can wade through the water, poking about with its beak for food.

Skinks eat spiders, insects and fruit, and will sometimes even eat food regurgitated by seabirds. Yuk! New Zealand has about 28 species, including the speckled skink, shore skink, small-scaled skink, southern skink, striped skink, scree skink, small-eared skink, spotted skink . . .

Shags live by the coast and dive into the sea to catch fish. Their feathers can soon become waterlogged, making it difficult for them to fly, so they perch with their wings held out until dry.

The New Zealand fur seal is our most common seal. It feeds mostly on fish, especially hoki. Seals have to be fast swimmers to catch fish, and some species have been clocked at 22–40km per hour!

Stick insects feed on lots of different plants, but if you search carefully you may see them on manuka. They have a funny, wobbly way of walking. Some tropical stick insects grow up to 350mm in length. The longest species in New Zealand measures 150mm from head to tail.

Moving at a top speed of 1 km an hour, it would take a stick insect 2–3 months to walk the length of New Zealand.

The starling is probably the most common wild bird of all. It's estimated that there are over 1 billion (1,000,000,000!) starlings around the world. Starlings were first introduced into New Zealand in 1862.

New Zealand's native veined slugs live mostly in bush and forest. Most are quite small, but some species can measure up to 150mm in length.

Slugs and snails like to eat all sorts of plant material, which is why gardeners don't like them. Garden snails are slow movers and travel at about 75mm per minute. At that rate it would take a garden snail nearly 42 years to travel the length of New Zealand.

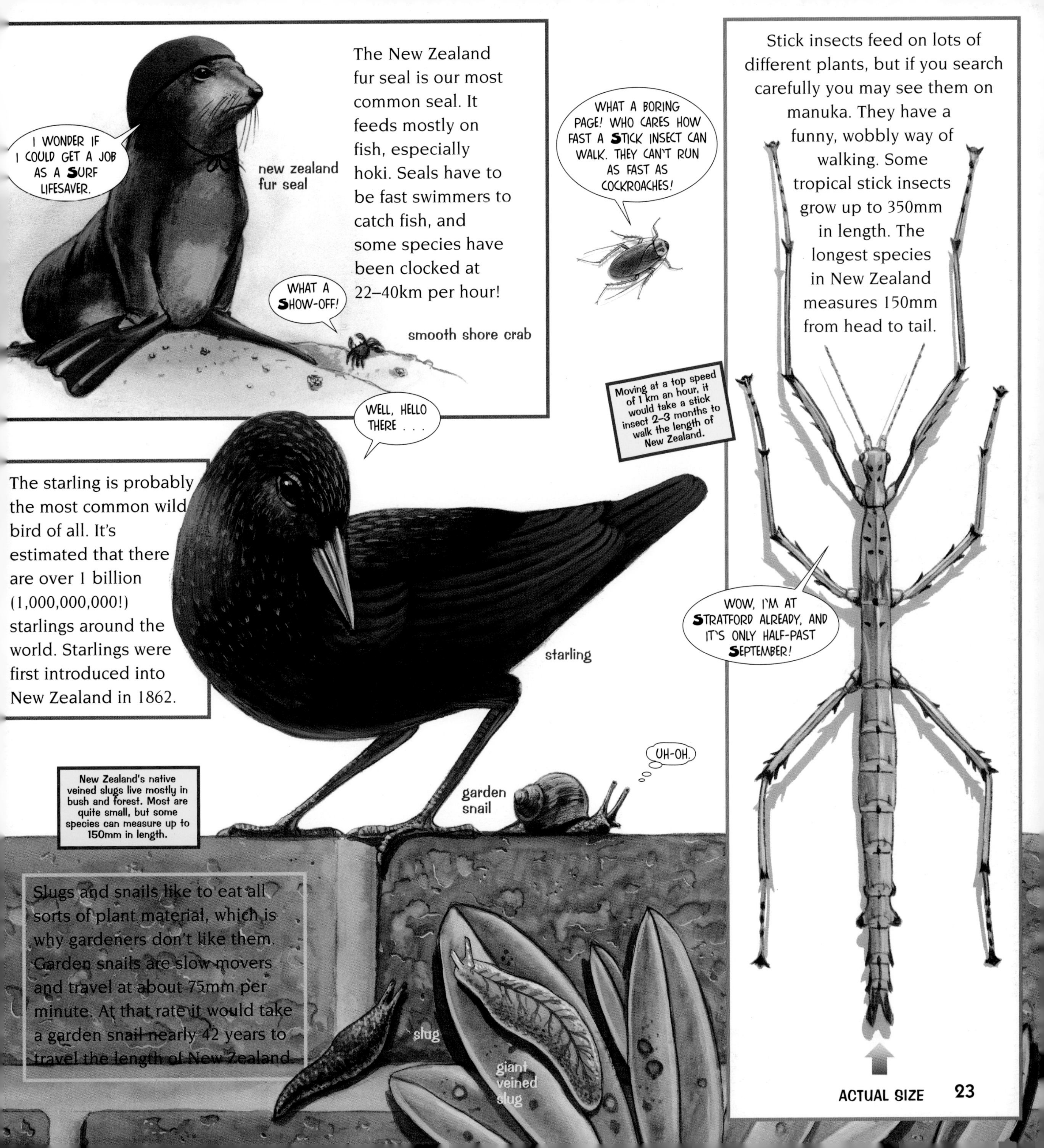

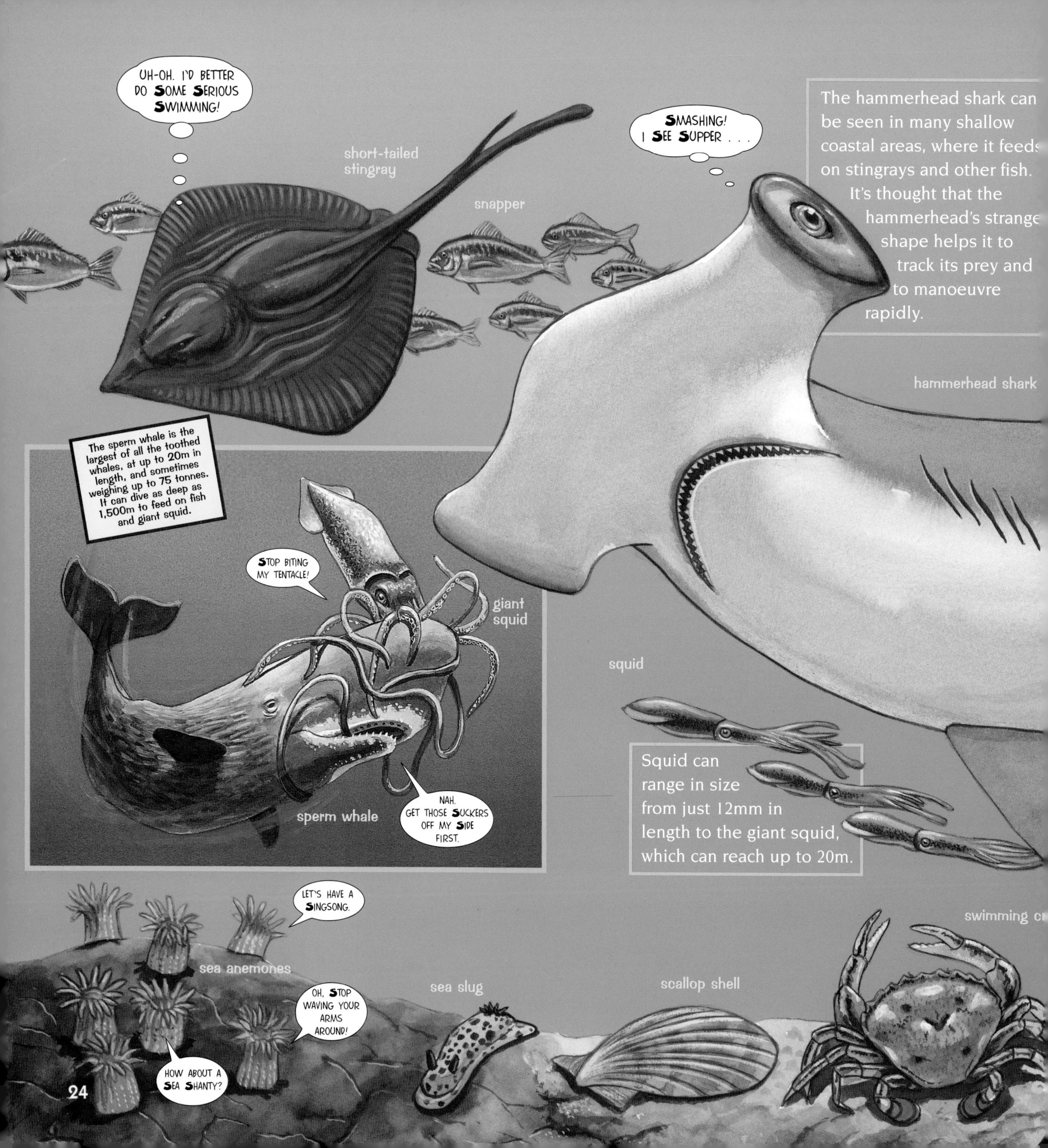
UH-OH. I'D BETTER DO SOME SERIOUS SWIMMING!
short-tailed stingray
snapper
SMASHING! I SEE SUPPER . . .
The hammerhead shark can be seen in many shallow coastal areas, where it feeds on stingrays and other fish. It's thought that the hammerhead's strange shape helps it to track its prey and to manoeuvre rapidly.
hammerhead shark
The sperm whale is the largest of all the toothed whales, at up to 20m in length, and sometimes weighing up to 75 tonnes. It can dive as deep as 1,500m to feed on fish and giant squid.
STOP BITING MY TENTACLE!
giant squid
NAH. GET THOSE SUCKERS OFF MY SIDE FIRST.
sperm whale
squid
Squid can range in size from just 12mm in length to the giant squid, which can reach up to 20m.
LET'S HAVE A SINGSONG.
sea anemones
OH, STOP WAVING YOUR ARMS AROUND!
HOW ABOUT A SEA SHANTY?
sea slug
scallop shell
swimming cr

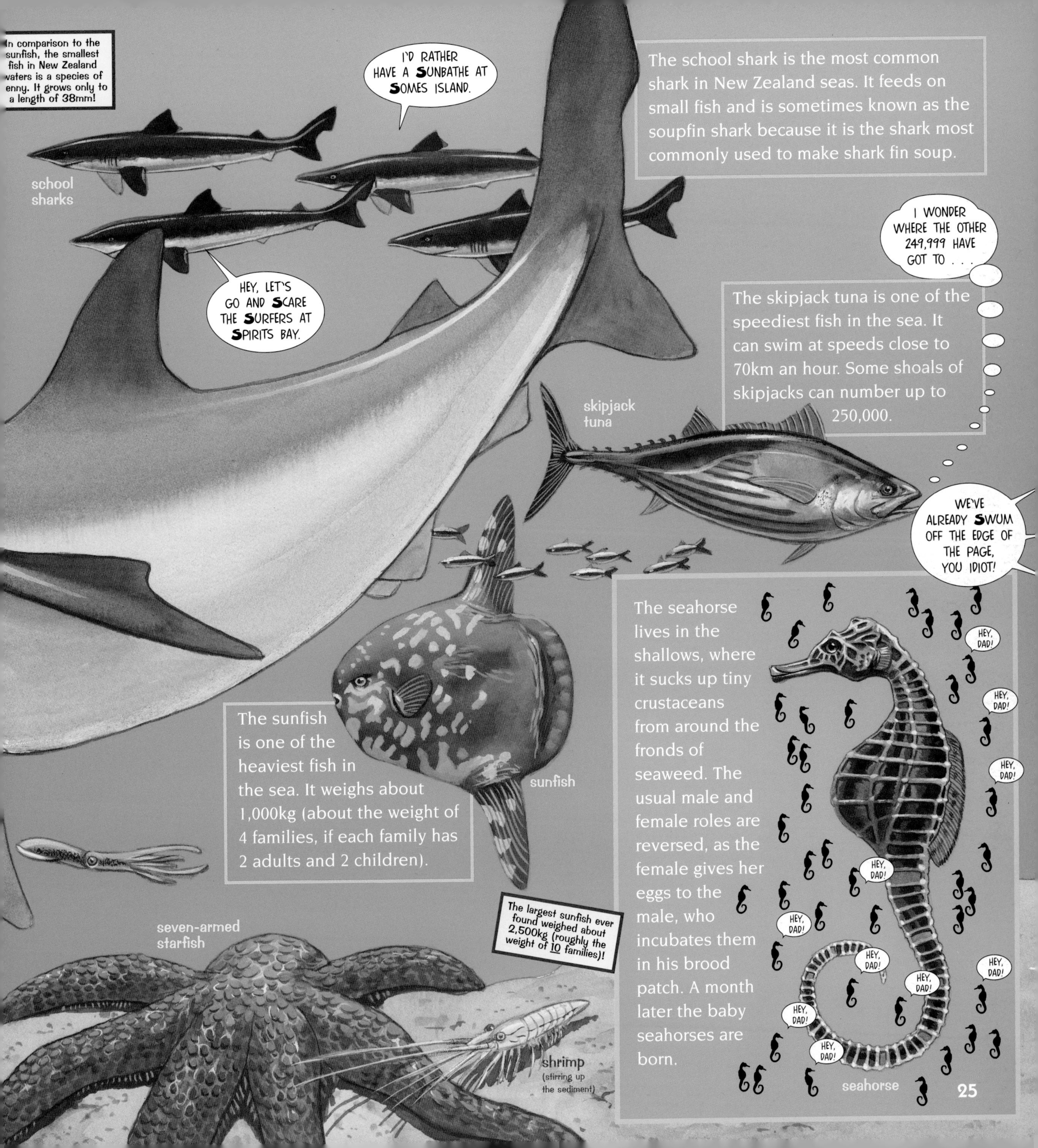

In comparison to the sunfish, the smallest fish in New Zealand waters is a species of enny. It grows only to a length of 38mm!

The school shark is the most common shark in New Zealand seas. It feeds on small fish and is sometimes known as the soupfin shark because it is the shark most commonly used to make shark fin soup.

The skipjack tuna is one of the speediest fish in the sea. It can swim at speeds close to 70km an hour. Some shoals of skipjacks can number up to 250,000.

The sunfish is one of the heaviest fish in the sea. It weighs about 1,000kg (about the weight of 4 families, if each family has 2 adults and 2 children).

The largest sunfish ever found weighed about 2,500kg (roughly the weight of 10 families)!

The seahorse lives in the shallows, where it sucks up tiny crustaceans from around the fronds of seaweed. The usual male and female roles are reversed, as the female gives her eggs to the male, who incubates them in his brood patch. A month later the baby seahorses are born.

The takahe was once thought to be extinct, but in 1948 it was 'rediscovered' in Fiordland. This flightless bird feeds on various plants, including tussock grasses, and lives for about 20 years.

The totara is another of our giant trees. It can reach as high as 30m, and grows so straight and regular that a Maori war canoe capable of holding over 100 men can be carved from a single totara trunk.

The tuatara's ancestors can be traced back more than 200 million years, to when the early dinosaurs were around. Tuataras can live for over 100 years. They feed on spiders, centipedes, slugs, snails, worms and insects, including wetas, and sometimes share their burrow with a seabird called a fairy prion.

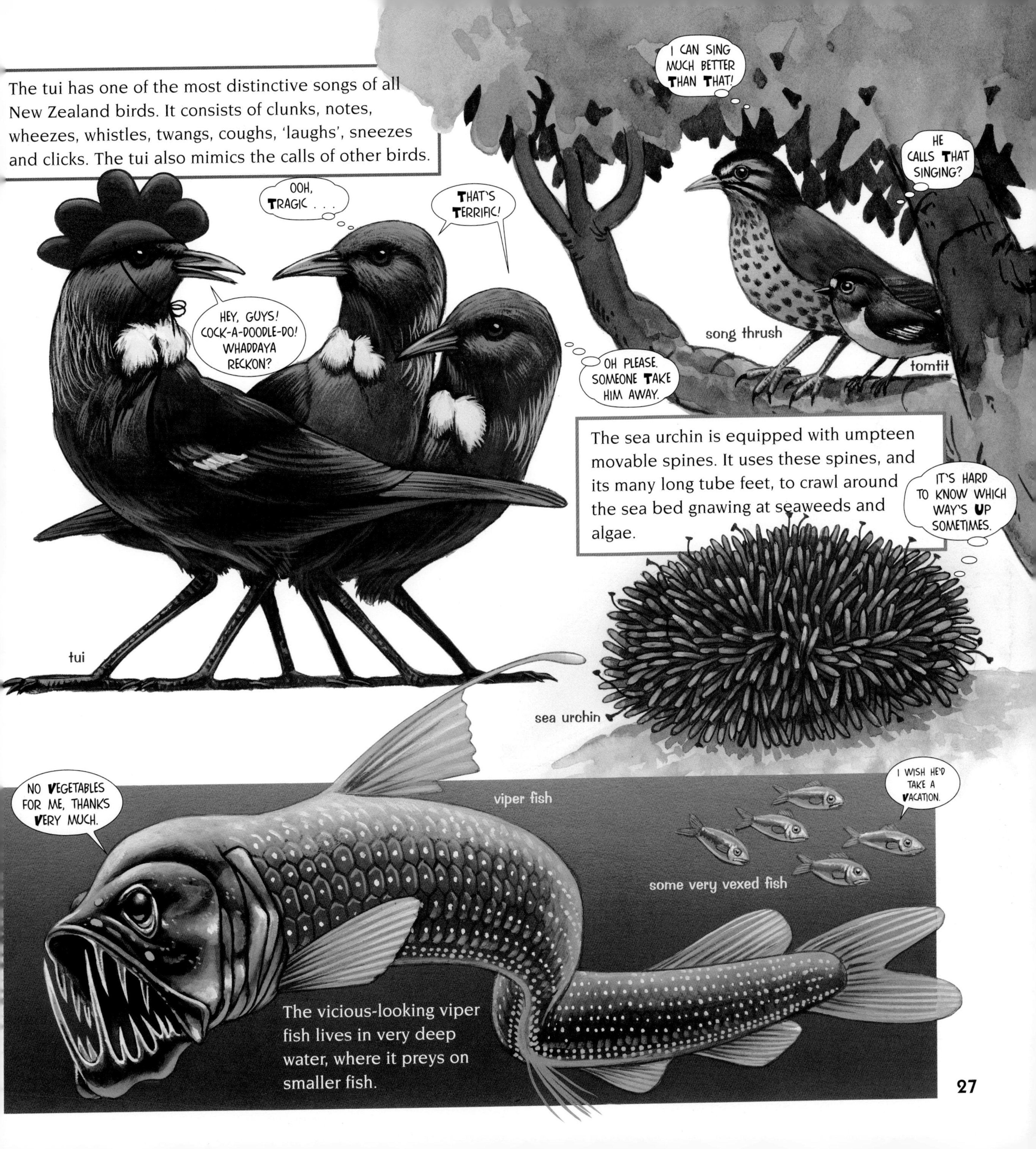
The tui has one of the most distinctive songs of all New Zealand birds. It consists of clunks, notes, wheezes, whistles, twangs, coughs, 'laughs', sneezes and clicks. The tui also mimics the calls of other birds.
I CAN SING MUCH BETTER THAN THAT!
HE CALLS THAT SINGING?
OOH, TRAGIC . . .
THAT'S TERRIFIC!
HEY, GUYS! COCK-A-DOODLE-DO! WHADDAYA RECKON?
OH PLEASE. SOMEONE TAKE HIM AWAY.
song thrush
tomtit
tui
The sea urchin is equipped with umpteen movable spines. It uses these spines, and its many long tube feet, to crawl around the sea bed gnawing at seaweeds and algae.
IT'S HARD TO KNOW WHICH WAY'S UP SOMETIMES.
sea urchin
NO VEGETABLES FOR ME, THANKS VERY MUCH.
viper fish
I WISH HE'D TAKE A VACATION.
some very vexed fish
The vicious-looking viper fish lives in very deep water, where it preys on smaller fish.

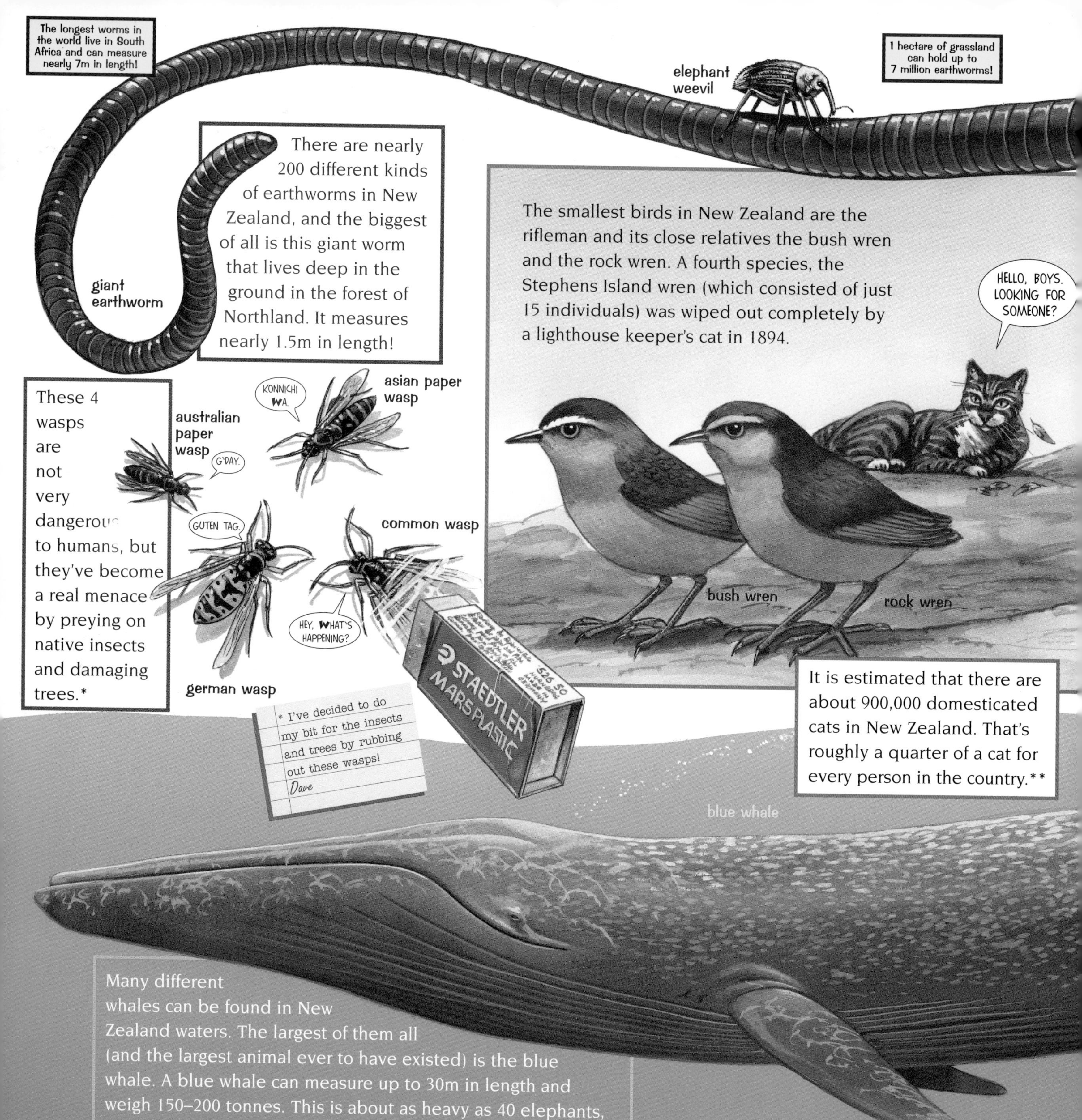

There are nearly 200 different kinds of earthworms in New Zealand, and the biggest of all is this giant worm that lives deep in the ground in the forest of Northland. It measures nearly 1.5m in length!

These 4 wasps are not very dangerous to humans, but they've become a real menace by preying on native insects and damaging trees.*

The smallest birds in New Zealand are the rifleman and its close relatives the bush wren and the rock wren. A fourth species, the Stephens Island wren (which consisted of just 15 individuals) was wiped out completely by a lighthouse keeper's cat in 1894.

It is estimated that there are about 900,000 domesticated cats in New Zealand. That's roughly a quarter of a cat for every person in the country.**

Many different whales can be found in New Zealand waters. The largest of them all (and the largest animal ever to have existed) is the blue whale. A blue whale can measure up to 30m in length and weigh 150–200 tonnes. This is about as heavy as 40 elephants, or 2,500 teachers, or 7,000 kids, or 1.5 million exercise books . . .

** Editor's note: Dave, don't be silly. Who'd want to have a quarter of a cat?

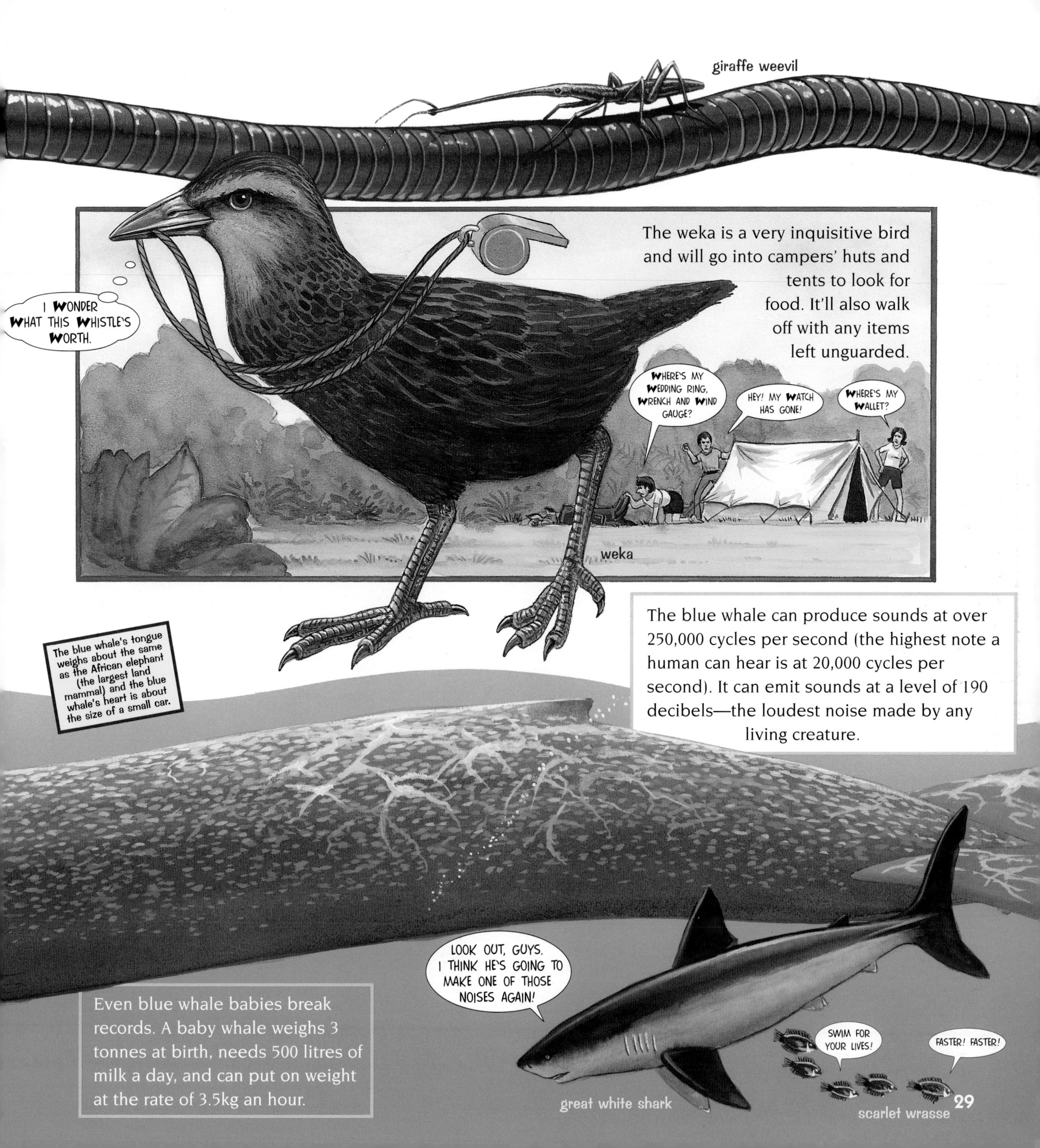

The weka is a very inquisitive bird and will go into campers' huts and tents to look for food. It'll also walk off with any items left unguarded.

The blue whale's tongue weighs about the same as the African elephant (the largest land mammal) and the blue whale's heart is about the size of a small car.

The blue whale can produce sounds at over 250,000 cycles per second (the highest note a human can hear is at 20,000 cycles per second). It can emit sounds at a level of 190 decibels—the loudest noise made by any living creature.

Even blue whale babies break records. A baby whale weighs 3 tonnes at birth, needs 500 litres of milk a day, and can put on weight at the rate of 3.5kg an hour.

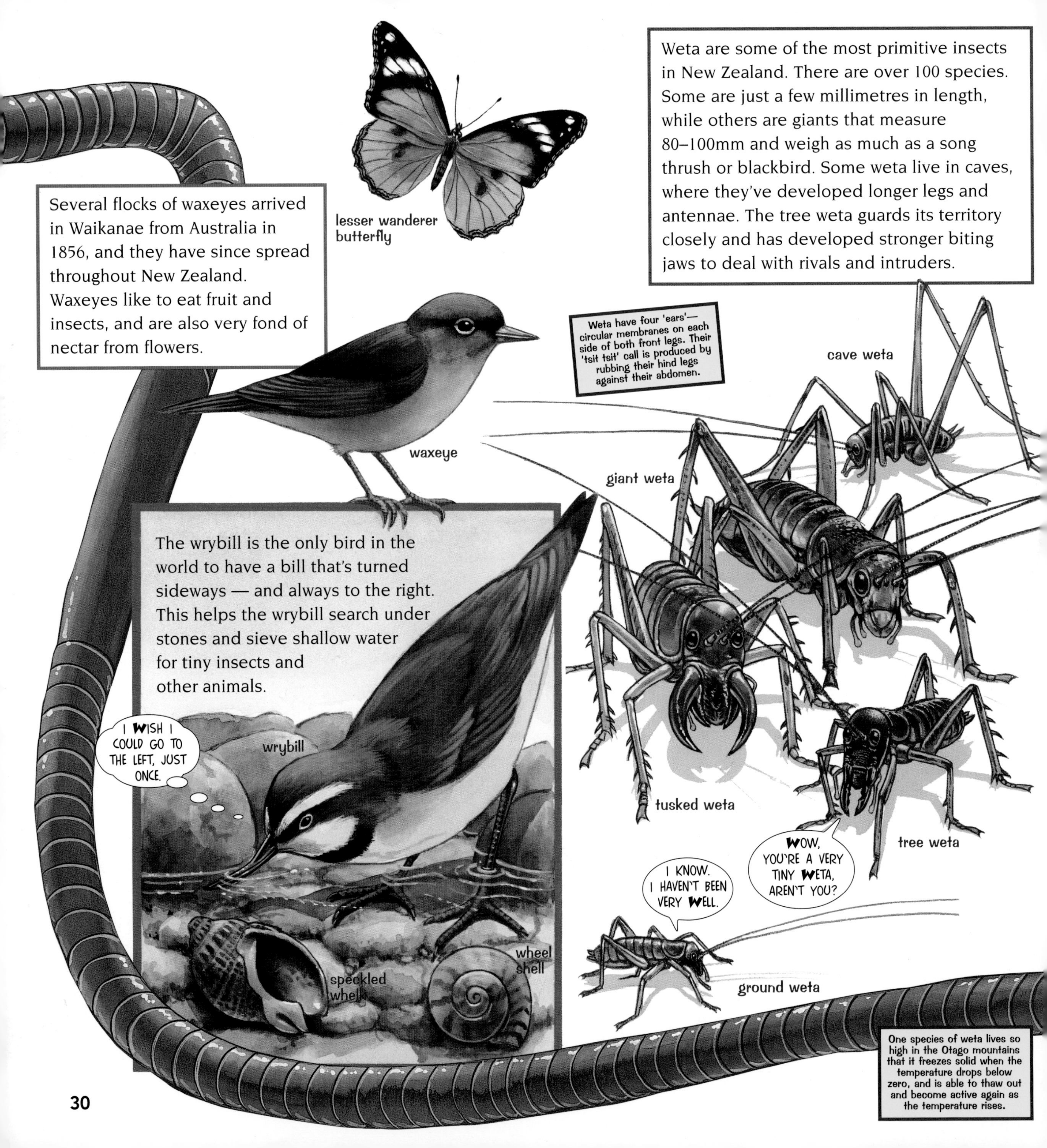

Weta are some of the most primitive insects in New Zealand. There are over 100 species. Some are just a few millimetres in length, while others are giants that measure 80–100mm and weigh as much as a song thrush or blackbird. Some weta live in caves, where they've developed longer legs and antennae. The tree weta guards its territory closely and has developed stronger biting jaws to deal with rivals and intruders.

Several flocks of waxeyes arrived in Waikanae from Australia in 1856, and they have since spread throughout New Zealand. Waxeyes like to eat fruit and insects, and are also very fond of nectar from flowers.

Weta have four 'ears'—circular membranes on each side of both front legs. Their 'tsit tsit' call is produced by rubbing their hind legs against their abdomen.

The wrybill is the only bird in the world to have a bill that's turned sideways — and always to the right. This helps the wrybill search under stones and sieve shallow water for tiny insects and other animals.

One species of weta lives so high in the Otago mountains that it freezes solid when the temperature drops below zero, and is able to thaw out and become active again as the temperature rises.

YAHOO!
yellow-crowned parakeet
YOU'RE LOOKING VERY YELLOW TODAY.
OH, YES!
YELLOWER THAN YESTERDAY?
YIPPEE!
yellow admiral butterfly
ALL THIS TALK ABOUT YELLOW IS MAKING ME QUEASY.
yellowhammer
yellowhead
yellow longhorn beetle
No animals in New Zealand have a name starting with X, so I've made a space for you to draw your very own species. (Practise on a spare piece of paper first, and don't forget to give it a name beginning with X!)
Dave
Seasnakes hold their breath underwater using tiny hinged scales that close off their nostrils. Some seasnakes are very poisonous, but these snakes are not very common in New Zealand waters.
yellow-bellied seasnake
Zooplankton is the name given to all the very tiny animals in the sea. Some of them are so small they're microscopic.
zigzag weed
yellow-banded perch
DON'T GET MUCH OF A FEATURE IN THIS ZANY BOOK, DO WE?
NAH, NOT EVEN ONE CLOSE-UP.

Editor's note: Oh, gross! Dave, do you reall
have to keep putting in this kind of thing?